NEW KIDS
ON THE BLOCK
Scrapbook

Grace Catalano

Designed by Joseph Catalano

A SIGNET BOOK

About The Author

GRACE CATALANO is the editor of three entertainment magazines, *Rock Legend*, and the popular teen magazines, *Dream Guys* and *Dream Guys Presents*. Her books include *New Kids on the Block*, *Kirk Cameron: Dream Guy*, *River Phoenix: Hero and Heartthrob*, *Alyssa Milano: She's The Boss* and *Teen Star Yearbook*. She also wrote *Elvis—A 10th Anniversary Tribute* and *Elvis and Priscilla*. Grace lives on the North Shore of Long Island.

Dedicated to Mom and Dad.

SIGNET
Published by the Penguin Group
Penguin Books USA Inc., 375 Hudson Street,
New York, New York 10014, U.S.A.
Penguin Books Ltd, 27 Wrights Lane,
London W8 5TZ, England
Penguin Books Australia Ltd., Ringwood,
Victoria, Australia
Penguin Books Canada Ltd, 2801 John Street,
Markham, Ontario, Canada L3R 1B4
Penguin Books (N.Z.) Ltd, 182-190 Wairau Road,
Auckland 10, New Zealand

Penguin Books Ltd, Registered Offices:
Harmondsworth, Middlesex, England

First published by Signet, an imprint of Penguin Books USA Inc.

First Printing, April, 1990
10 9 8 7 6 5 4 3 2

Photo Credits: Celebrity Photo, London Features, Ebet Roberts, Star File, Janet Macoska, Michele Hoffman, Columbia Records.

CONTENTS

INTRODUCTION

In the history of pop/rock music, few bands have ever equaled the meteoric rise to fame of New Kids on the Block. Since their second album, *Hangin' Tough*, was released in early 1989, the New Kids found themselves on a road leading them to the top.

The group, which includes brothers Jon and Jordan Knight, Donnie Wahlberg, Joe McIntyre and Danny Wood, admit their overnight success is mind-boggling, but very gratifying.

"I think it's great," says Jon. "The odds of this actually happening are astronomical."

Even more astronomical are the statistics surrounding New Kids on the Block. Everyday seems to bring a new milestone to the band as they keep breaking records set by some of the world's most successful groups.

The New Kids became the first act since The Beatles to have the top two entries on the Hot 100 in the same week with their singles *Cover Girl* and *Didn't I (Blow Your Mind)*.

They became the first teen group *ever* to

have a number one album and single on the charts simultaneously.

With two number one singles released in a row, the New Kids were the first teen group since the Jackson 5 in 1970 to have back-to-back number one singles.

No other teen group since the Jackson 5 has ever had an album reach the top five Hot 100 chart position.

The New Kids are the first teen group in music history to have four Top 10 singles off one album.

There's no doubt about it—New Kids-mania is sweeping the country. They have taken the world by storm with their chart-topping music and terrific dance moves. In songs like *Hangin' Tough,* the guys say they are trying to convey messages to their many fans.

"That song says go out and do what you've got to do, just hang tough," says Jon. "Don't let anybody get in your way of anything you want to do."

That may explain why these Kids have become so popular. The group, which was formed in 1984, worked long and hard to achieve success. For a while, it didn't seem like they would ever get to the top. But drive and determination kept them going. And their second album, *Hangin' Tough,* turned them into the superstars they are today. The New Kids are proving to be a mainstay in the music world.

In between their busy schedules, the guys find time to speak out to their fans on the dangers of drug abuse and are the teen spokesmen for the United Cerebral Palsy organization.

"I think our success gives other kids role models, positive role models," says Jordan. "Because we don't do drugs or things like that. I think that's important. "

The New Kids are so popular that when New York's Z100 radio station held a concert ticket giveaway contest, winners had a choice between going to see New Kids on the Block or The Rolling Stones. Eighty percent chose the New Kids.

Jon, Jordan, Joe, Donnie and Danny, five talented guys from Boston, are riding the crest of an immense wave of popularity that seems to be getting stronger everyday.

Part One

MEET NEW KIDS ON THE BLOCK

"Jordan is real smooth on stage," says Donnie. "Like glass, his dancing, his vocals. He has got a world of talent."

JORDAN KNIGHT

"We've noticed that as the New Kids became popular, we all found out we had friends we never had before. They are only friends with us now while we're popular. A true friend to me is someone who will be there when the chips are down!"
—**Jordan**

Tall, dark and handsome Jordan Nathaniel Marcel Knight was born on May 17, 1971 in Worcester, Massachusetts. As a young boy, Jordan grew up surrounded by music, but never thought of going into music professionally. Before he was fifteen years old, Jordan's only exposure to performing was singing with his brothers and sisters in the church choir.

"He was more into breakdancing than singing," says his mom, Marlene. "Jordan was with a youth organization near our home and put on breakdancing shows and demonstrations. He also taught kids how to breakdance."

At age fourteen, Jordan tried out for a new band, New Kids on the Block and was surprised that he was chosen. He wrestled with a lot of emotions whether to continue breakdancing or give it up to rehearse every day with the band. "I wasn't sure what would be the right thing to do," he says.

What changed Jordan's mind was that his older brother, Jon, was also selected as a member of the band. "I think I would go crazy if Jon weren't in the group with me," Jordan honestly admits. "The great part about it is that whenever I need to ask Jon something, he's always ready to listen."

Jordan chose to give his time to New Kids on the Block and rehearsed with them everyday after school. Some days, all five New Kids would rehearse in the Knight family's basement.

After being a New Kid for one year, Jordan was convinced that he really wanted to be part of it. He realized how much the world of music really meant to him. He began writing songs and singing lead with the band. He also became interested in playing the electronic keyboard.

"Jordan never took formal piano lessons," says his mom. "I bought him a keyboard when he joined the group. He played on our old piano, but after he became involved with the band, he really discovered the keyboard. From that point on, I would hear him playing music in his bedroom every minute he was not in school."

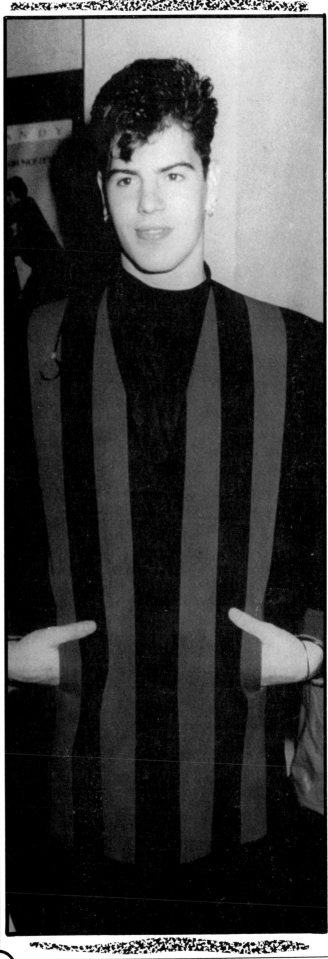

Jordan gets very emotional when he sings. His energy never ends!

Jordan's determination made New Kids producer Maurice Starr take special notice of him. Danny explains that Starr gives Jordan many of the new tunes first. "When a song first comes up, our producer will usually come to us and say, 'Jordan, check this out, I want you to sing this," says Danny. "And then if someone else can sing it better, we'll change singers."

Danny, who writes songs with Jordan, adds that he is one of the most dedicated New Kids. He's constantly thinking up new ideas for songs because he loves to create.

For Jordan, his favorite time is singing onstage and writing music. "When we're traveling, I like to bring my little keyboards with me on the road, so I can keep up with my practicing and write some songs," he says. "I have a few songs that I wrote that will probably be on our next album."

Jordan is so involved with music that when he isn't writing songs, recording or singing his heart out onstage, he likes to listen to music on the stereo. He says it's the perfect remedy for relaxing and unwinding after a grueling day.

In the past year, Jordan hasn't had too much time to call his own. He's been on a hectic tour schedule with the New Kids. So, when he comes off the road, he likes to

spend some time alone in his room. There are times Jordan just likes to think everything through. "I like to get my head straight from all the chaos," he says.

While Jordan is on the right track concerning his career, there are times he reflects about how life has changed for him over these past four years. The band has become so recognizable that they find it difficult to do everyday things, like go to the mall or to a movie. "We used to be able to hang out like normal guys," he says. "But now everyone stares. It can make us a little self-conscious. We don't have as much free time anymore. Our lives are real hectic."

All the traveling Jordan does has cut into his social life. He had a girlfriend in high school, but he doesn't have the time right now to devote to dating.

He feels it wouldn't be fair to a girl if he only saw her when his schedule permitted. But Jordan knows exactly the kind of girl he likes. "She has to be loving, independent and have a great sense of humor," he offers. "But it's difficult to date anyone because girls know me as part of New Kids on the Block and ask, 'So where are the other four guys?'"

Personally, Jordan is looking forward to meeting his ideal girl and settling down someday, but he's in no hurry. He's too serious about his music and giving as much as he can to the band.

His future dreams are to continue on the same musical road he's on right now. "In the years ahead, I see us writing more of our own material," he says, "and playing more instruments. I'm studying the guitar and the other guys have all been practicing instruments."

Jordan realizes that someday he may not be part of the band anymore. "When that day comes, I'll go into something else," he says. "I have a lot that I'd like to do. I plan on becoming a record producer, songwriter and maybe even a solo artist!"

For someone as talented as Jordan Knight, the possibilities are endless!

The gorgeous Knight brothers, Jordan and Jon love being in the band together. "It's great knowing my brother is there when I need him," says Jordan and Jon feels the same way.

Q and A with Jordan Knight

Q: Who was the first girl Jordan dated?
A: At thirteen years old, Jordan went out on his first date with a girl named Pam. He had never kissed a girl before and says, "I didn't know how to. But we worked it out." Soonafter, Pam went to summer camp and left Jordan for another boy. "I got over it," smiles brown-eyed Jordan. "It was cool."

Q: What advice would Jordan give to kids who want to go into show business?
A: Jordan says, "Anyone who wants to get into show business should go for it. But you have to know that it is tough. You have to be lucky because even if you're talented and work hard, there's still a chance that you won't get anywhere. You have to make sure you believe in yourself and you have to have friends who you can turn to during the letdowns."

Q: What are Jordan's feelings about being in New Kids on the Block?
A: "I really enjoy being in the group," states Jordan. "I'll admit rehearsals can be boring, but it's fun, and it's a great opportunity. The neighborhood we come from is rough. We see a lot of people just hanging out and some are on drugs. That's why I thank our producer for taking us under his wing and working with us, getting us into music. He's the one who brought us here, and we'll stick with him to the end."

Q: Do the New Kids ever fight?
A: Like all close friends, the guys occasionally have an argument. "We fight," says Jordan, "but we get over it. If everything was perfect, then something would probably be wrong."

Q: How long did it take Jordan to grow his long braid?
A: About five years ago, Jordan started to let a piece of his hair in the back grow out long. But, he says, some day soon he wants to cut it off.

Q: What is Jordan's secret wish?
A: The thing that would make Jordan very happy is "If there would be no more war and there was only peace in the world."

Q: Has Jordan ever tried to disguise himself so fans wouldn't recognize him?
A: Jordan admits that he tried a few disguises, but none have worked. "When we were in Cleveland, Joe and I tried disguising ourselves as hot dog vendors. We put on outfits and started walking through the park. It worked for a second, but only for a second. I'm trying to find out where Michael Jackson gets his disguises," grins Jordan.

•JORDAN'S •FACT FILE

Full Real Name: Jordan Nathaniel Marcel Knight
Nickname: "J"
Birthdate: May 17, 1971
Birthplace: Worcester, Massachusetts
Hair: Dark brown
Eyes: Brown
Height: 5′10″
Weight: 155 lbs.
Shoe Size: 10½
Shirt Size: Large
Parents: Marlene and Allan

Brothers & Sisters: Allison, Sharon, David, Chris, fellow New Kid Jon
Pets: Siamese cats, Buster and Misty
First Job: Camp counselor
Instrument Played: Keyboards
Most Prized Possessions: "My family and friends."
Favorite Food: Lasagna, Italian, Chinese, Northside Burgers
Favorite Drink: Chocolate milkshake
Favorite City: Boston, Massachusetts
Favorite Pastime: Going to the beach
Favorite Book: *Jonathan Livingston Seagull*
Favorite Play: *Julius Caesar*
Favorite Actor: Robert DeNiro
Favorite TV Shows: *The Cosby Show, America's Most Wanted*
Favorite Movies: *Soul Man, Robocop, The Untouchables*
Favorite Song: *You Make Me Feel Brand New* by The Stylistics
Favorite Hobbies: Going to clubs, reading magazines
Favorite Sports: Basketball, swimming
Favorite Childhood Memory: "Singing in the church choir."
Favorite Type of Girl: A loving girl who likes to have fun.
Favorite Type of Date: "On a secluded beach at night with a fire."
Favorite Vacation Spot: Hawaii
Favorite Color: Blue
Favorite Type of Clothes: "Hip, street stuff."
Self-Description: "I am a person who likes everything I do to be perfect. I don't worry too much. I don't get excited. I always look on the bright side of things. I'm creative, loving and caring."
Biggest Thrill: "Hearing a New Kids song on the radio for the first time."
Biggest Disappointment: "Having that same song flop."
Message To Fans: "Keep faith in the New Kids and we will always be there for you."
Where To Write To Jordan:
Jordan Knight
c/o New Kids on the Block
Columbia Records
51 West 52nd Street
New York, NY 10019

JON KNIGHT

"A lot of fans send us teddy bears and stuffed animals and they want to know what we do with all of them. At home in my closet, I have a case of about 5000 teddy bears."
—Jon

Soft-spoken Jonathan Rashleigh Knight has the reputation of being the most organized New Kid. "Jon really loves helping people," reveals his younger brother and fellow band mate

"I think it's nice that so many kids are looking up to us. I want the group to be a role model to young people."
—Jon

Jordan Knight. "I think that's why Jon is always looking after all of us in the group, making sure things run smoothly."

Jon, who was born on November 29, 1968, was raised in a very loving and unusual household. "I was brought up never to judge other people," he explains. "My mother would let foster kids stay with us. I have an adopted brother who is black and sometimes people ask me how I feel about that. I think it's great because I learned how to get along with all kinds of people."

Prior to joining the band, Jon talked about going into real estate development. He was always interested in building things and likes watching the PBS TV show *This Old House* for ideas.

There are many different sides to Jon and he has many different interests. His wide range of favorites go from watching old Mickey Mouse cartoons to the TV show *thirtysomething*. A genuinely honest and down-to-earth guy, Jon loves to ski and swim and date as often as he can.

"I like a girl who is fun to be with and easy to talk to," he says. He doesn't list any particularly special place to go on a date except to say, "As long as you're with the one you love, it doesn't matter where you go or what you do."

Jon never goes anywhere without his dog, Nikko.

Jon, who always dresses up, was happy when it was decided the New Kids would wear new stage outfits. "Before we kind of roughed it. It was pretty much up to us how to dress," he says. "But now we have a guy who designs our clothes for the shows. I think it was a terrific step up for the band."

Jon is having a great time being part of the most successful group of the year. He especially likes meeting the band's legion of fans. "It does get a little crazy sometimes," he says. "And even a little scary. I was trapped in an elevator with a mob of girls. It's like they want a piece of you. Because we have kids as our fans, it's probably like the first group that they've had a crush on. I think it's nice that so many kids are looking up to us."

Jon puts all his energy into every New Kids concert, perfecting his dance steps. He admires the dance moves of the old Motown groups and has tried to duplicate some of their steps. "They were great," he says with a smile. "I think my moves are like the old stuff, but I like to step with a little more energy."

Even though the New Kids have been performing all over the world, Jon still struggles with bouts of stage fright.

"We've been doing so many concerts, I'm getting used to it now," he says. "But there are days when I look out and see all those people and I do feel nervous."

Jon is still learning to adjust to being in the spotlight, but says a career in music is his primary future interest. If one day he was no longer a performer, Jon plans on working behind-the-scenes.

He'd like to manage a band someday. "I'd like to be able to give advice and watch out for a new group," he confides. "I've been there and I want to pass on what I've learned to a.band of my own."

As a New Kid, Jon feels like the band has done some good for other teenagers. Not only have they made some great music, but the group has become a role model to young people. And Jon feels that is the most important thing of all.

Q & A with Jon Knight

Q: What has Jon done with the money he's earned?

A: Two things Jon has bought have been presents for his loving mom, Marlene. He surprised her with a brand new Lincoln Continental car with a customized license plate which reads: "4 U MA!" Even though that gift was very generous, the Knight brothers decided to surprise their mother with something more special. Jon and Jordan pooled their money and bought their mom a new house. "Jordan and I have been looking for a while and we finally decided on one we like," says Jon. "It's so pretty. It's on a hill and is surrounded by great big trees. It has a view of the Atlantic Ocean." The new Knight residence will also be home to Jon, Jordan and all their brothers, sisters, nieces and nephews. "We're all grown up, but we want to stay together," says Jon. "Jordan and I are going to turn the attic into an apartment and live up there, and the rest of the family can have the remainder of the house."

Q: Why doesn't Jon sing alone during the New Kids concerts?

A: He just doesn't feel ready for it yet. He is only recently beginning to record one solo number on each of New Kids on the Block's albums. Everyone loved his rendition of *White Christmas* on the New Kids' *Merry, Merry Christmas* album. As for singing live in concert, Jon says, "I just can't picture myself singing all alone onstage! It was hard enough to get me to do it in the studio."

Q: How do the other New Kids describe Jon?

A: Donnie says of his fellow bandmate, "Jon is the shyest. His personality onstage is very shy. Musically he is like a blend. He just blends so well in the harmonies. But he comes across shy and the girls really like that." Jon's younger brother, Jordan, has this to say about him: "Jon worries a lot. He's the businessman of the group. I think he'd be a great manager when he gets older. He's super efficient. If things aren't going right, he'll take it in his own hands."

Q: How did Jon feel when Governor Michael Dukakis declared April 24, 1989 "New Kids on the Block Day"?

A: Jon and the rest of the kids were very excited on that day. "It made us feel we had accomplished something," says Jon. "At the time we thought if we're considered role models and kids are looking up to us, we might as well use our power to do something positive in the world. We were very honored that the Governor felt he should recognize us for what we've been doing with his and other anti-drug organizations."

Jon's Fact File

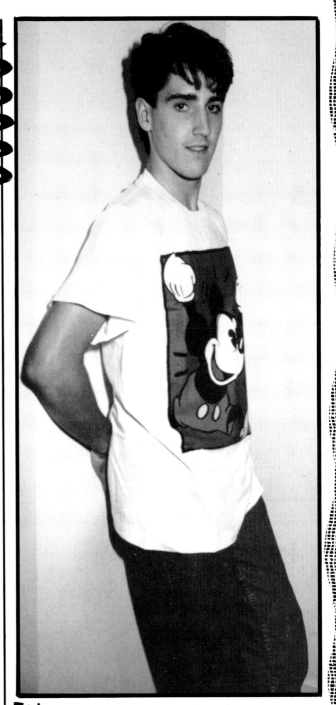

Full Real Name: Jonathan Rashleigh Knight

Birthdate: November 29, 1968

Birthplace: Worcester, Massachusetts

Hair: Brown

Eyes: Hazel

Height: 5'11"

Weight: 155 lbs.

Shoe Size: 10½

Shirt Size: Large

Parents: Marlene Putnam and Allan Knight

Brothers & Sisters: Allison, Sharon, David, Chris, fellow New Kid Jordan

Most Memorable Moment: "Hearing a New Kids song on the radio for the first time."

First Record Bought: "I don't know. Probably *Mickey Mouse Sings*," he says.

Biggest Influence On His Life: "My mom because she taught me to be a good person."

Favorite City: "Boston because it's home and home is the best place to be."

Favorite Sports: Skiing, swimming

Favorite TV Shows: *The Cosby Show*, *thirtysomething*

Favorite Food: Italian

Favorite Fast Food: Burger King

Favorite Junk Food: Chocolate and Hostess Cupcakes

Favorite Drink: Chocolate and strawberry milkshakes

Favorite Colors: Black and white

Favorite Childhood Memory: "Spending summers at my grandparents cottage in Canada."

Favorite Music: R&B and Pop

Favorite Type of Girl: "Someone who is independent, honest, sweet and smart. I like someone I can talk to and is fun to be with."

Favorite Car: Black BMW 735

Favorite School Subjects: Science and art

Pet Peeves: Heavy metal music, eggs, war and indifferences

Message To Fans: "Love yourself and others so we can make our world a better place."

Secret Wish: "For everyone to be happy!"

Where To Write To Jon:
Jon Knight
c/o New Kids on the Block
Columbia Records
51 West 52nd Street
New York, NY 10019

JOE McINTYRE

> "In hotels, it's easier to fall asleep because you know someone else is in the room with you. When you have your own room, it's so empty so I leave the TV on."
>
> —Joe

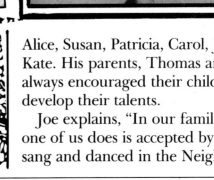

Blue-eyed Joseph Mulrey McIntyre is the youngest member of New Kids on the Block. Born on December 31, 1972 in Needham, Massachusetts, Joe has always been involved in performing. The baby of the McIntyre family, Joe has one brother, Tom, and seven sisters, Judith, Alice, Susan, Patricia, Carol, Jean and Kate. His parents, Thomas and Kay, always encouraged their children to develop their talents.

Joe explains, "In our family, whatever one of us does is accepted by the others. I sang and danced in the Neighborhood

Children Theater of Boston since I was six years old. I played the lead role in the musical play *Oliver* and in one show, my whole family sang the opening song. All except my dad who sat in the back watching. I really feel that those early years of performing nurtured me for the New Kids."

The McIntyre children were so talented, they participated in many community plays. "Even before I joined New Kids, my family was well-known around my neighborhood," says Joe.

Holidays were always fun in Joe's house. "We'd perform for our relatives who came over the house," he recalls."My brother and me used to pull out our tennis rackets and make believe we were playing guitars, pretending to be rock stars."

Now that Joe really *is* a rock star, he doesn't have as much time to spend at home. As part of New Kids on the Block, he has been moving in perpetual motion living a very hectic life on the road. But this happy kid wouldn't trade in his success for anything!

"We're really enjoying the success we've achieved as New Kids on the Block," offers Joe. "There weren't any groups like us. Young black kids could look up to New Edition and there was Menudo. But there wasn't a young white group that could be a good role model for teens. We've been very luck that we were given the chance. If there are a million people in the music business, there are two million more waiting to get in."

Joe is having a great time performing in

Joe McIntyre is the youngest New Kid and also the baby of his family.

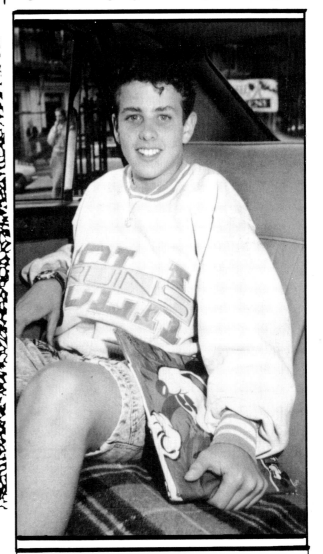

Oooh . . . Joe is so mesmerizing!

the band. "We're like brothers," he says of his friendship with Donnie, Jordan, Jon and Danny. "And I think that's why we're so popular with teens. They can tell by our chemistry onstage that we're having a good time. So they have a good time, too."

Even though he loves being part of the group, Joe does admit that the traveling and living out of a suitcase does get tiring. His mom understands this and lets her son relax when he gets home from tour.

"My mom will usually let me off from my usual chores around the house when I come home after I've been away a while," he says. "She also lets me spend as much time as I need to chill out with my friends."

What does Joe miss the most about leaving home? "I guess my bedroom. The thing I look forward to is coming home and sleeping in my own bed."

Joe is quick to list all the fun stuff he likes to do that he can't do while on tour. "I never have time to just sit back and flick on a TV" he says. "And of course, I like playing basketball, football and baseball. When we're traveling, we usually go from the bus to the hotel room to the stage."

Joe also likes catching up on his reading, especially indulging in a good mystery. And his favorite hobby of all is playing golf. "I love the game," he says. "It's really very relaxing, but challenging at the same time."

This New Kid certainly knows what makes him happy and at the top of his list is singing his heart out for his loving fans. "Sometimes I have to tell myself not to think of home," he confides. "I have to put everything aside and just work!"

So, for now, home for Joe and the rest of the New Kids is a bus, traveling from concert to concert. "In 10 years, we might not be together as New Kids on the Block," says Joe. "But I think we will all continue in the music business, either producing, managing or going out on our own. We take it as it comes, but for now it's New Kids on the Block."

One smile from Joe is all it takes to send his female fans screaming!

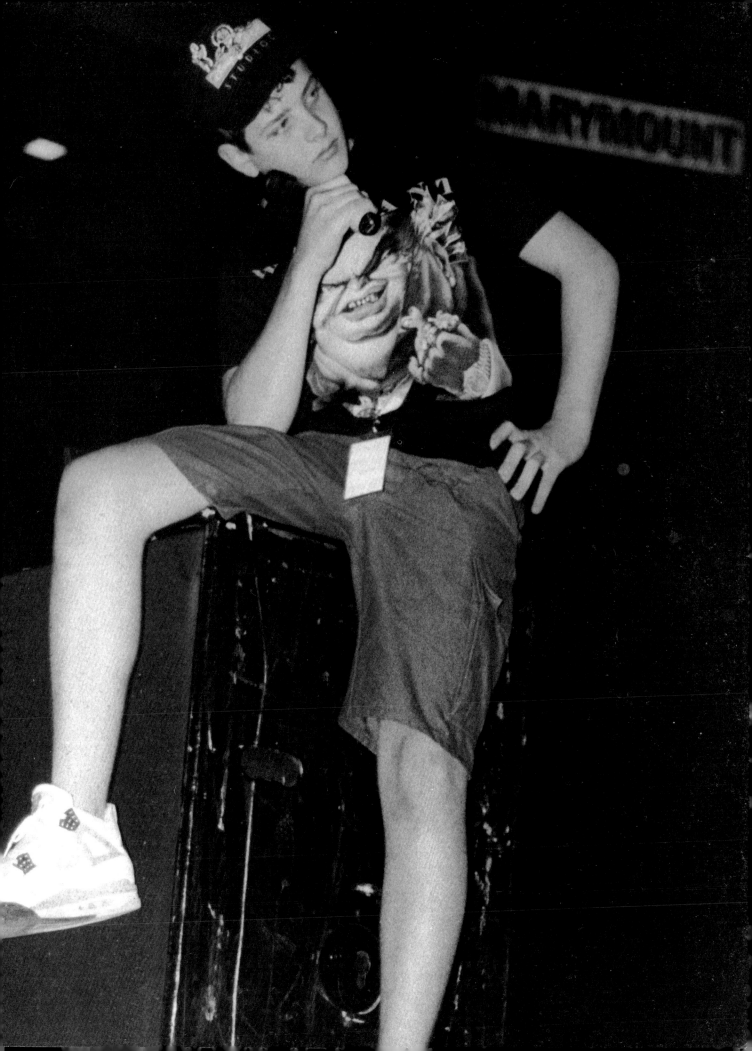

Q and A with Joe McIntyre

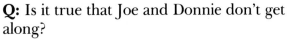

Q: Is it true that Joe and Donnie don't get along?

A: No, these kids are quite close. It was a little rough for Joe when he first joined the band because he was younger than the rest of the guys. "We didn't accept Joe at first," says Donnie, "because our good friend was leaving. We didn't know Joe because he was from a different neighborhood. He looked kind of square and we weren't sure if he was going to fit in. But I started to realize what a great guy Joe is. I look at him now and I see a younger version of myself." Joe says, "It's funny because sometimes Donnie and I get on a roll and it's non-stop arguing. But other times neither of us will say anything back. We are good friends."

Q: How does Joe feel about performing in concert?

A: Joe regards the concerts as the best part of being in the group. "I like performing because I think you get the full effect of all your hard work," he says. "It's the time to get the feedback from the audience and see how you really are doing with them and the music."

Q: Does Joe feel like he missed out on anything in his life because he joined the band at age twelve?

A: Joe honestly admits, "Sometimes I feel that I missed parts of growing up, being a teen and going to high school. Before we started touring, I was almost the perfect student. I did all my homework and had fun in school. Then all that suddenly changed. I'm always around adults. It's not always fun. Sometimes I'd rather be home playing sports with my friends. But I really enjoy being in this band. I've become close friends with the other guys. I never mind not being able to chill out at home with my friends because I can still chill out with Donnie, Danny, Jon and Jordan."

Q: What kind of girl does Joe like and what is his idea of a dream date?

A: Joe says, "I'm not really looking for a girlfriend right now. But if a girl catches my eye, I'll talk to her. I'd like to meet someone who is independent and has her own personality. Someone cool, chill and smart." As for the best place to take his girl, Joe enthuses, "Disneyland without a doubt. It's the ultimate. With all those rides and exhibits, you can't miss having a good time!"

JOE'S FACT FILE

Full Real Name: Joseph Mulrey McIntyre
Nicknames: Joe Bird, Joey Joe

Birthdate: December 31, 1972
Birthplace: Needham, Massachusetts
Hair: Blondish brown
Eyes: Blue
Height: 5'6"
Weight: 120 lbs.
Shoe Size: 8½
Shirt Size: Small
Parents: Thomas and Kay
Brothers & Sisters: Judith, Alice, Susan, Patricia, Carol, Jean, Kate, Tom
Pet: A dog named Boe
Favorite Actors: Bill Cosby, Robert DeNiro
Favorite Actress: His sister, Judith
Favorite Movies: *Big, Beverly Hills Cop, Midnight Run*
Favorite TV Shows: *Cheers, Monday Night Football*
Favorite Bands: Huey Lewis and the News, The Temptations
Favorite Food: Mexican
Favorite Drink: Classic Coke
Favorite Clothes: "Anything comfortable!"
Favorite Car: BMW 325 with phone
Favorite Colors: Blue, red
Favorite Sports: Golf, basketball, football
Favorite Childhood Memory: "Christmas days with my family and taking a walk with my sister in the snow."
Biggest Influence On His Life: His family and friends
Musical Instrument Played: He's studying the piano
Hobby: Bowling
Main Goals: "To be rich and famous, but, most of all, to have peace of mind."
Ideal Girl: "Cool, chill, smart, independent and charming."
Ideal Date: Go to a movie and dinner
Self-Description: "Funny, peaceful, worried and chill."
Best Quality: "I'm smart."
Worst Quality: "I can't stand losing."
Most Prized Possession: His family
Where To Write To Joe:
    Joe McIntyre
    c/o New Kids on the Block
    Columbia Records
    51 West 52nd Street
    New York, NY 10019

DONNIE WAHLBERG

> *"I always wanted to be the center of attention. But I didn't dream about becoming a singer or anything. I had too much to worry about living day to day."*
> —Donnie

Donnie doesn't like riding ferris wheels. "I can ride everything else," he says, "but I hate ferris wheels. I think they are so dangerous."

Donald E. Wahlberg, Jr. describes himself as "very unpredictable. I always defend myself and my rights. I'm wild and crazy, but very lovable."

Donnie, who was the first to be signed to New Kids on the Block, was born on August 17, 1969 in Dorchester, Massachusetts to Donald, Sr. and Alma. Donnie has five brothers, Paul, Jim, Arthur, Bob and Mark and three sisters, Michelle, Debbie and Tracey.

He grew up in a rough neighborhood. "My family had a bad reputation and I was

a pretty wild kid myself," he says. "But people can't put me down by saying, 'You were a bad kid when you were younger.' I never said I wasn't. But I'm good now. We're clean, but we're clean by choice. Now, as part of the New Kids, I'm very positive, trying to educate kids."

Donnie was always interested in music, but he never thought of pursuing a career in show business. Instead, he worked several part-time jobs during his early teenage years. He helped his dad drive a truck delivering food to schools and summer camps. He also worked in a bank in downtown Boston and won an award for never missing a day.

In those early years, Donnie was a very realistic thinker. "I guess everyone dreams about being a star," he says. "But where I grew up, that was really farfetched."

At the age of ten, Donnie discovered music. He formed a band with two friends called Risk and practiced everyday after school. His mom, Alma, remembers, "Right around the time he was becoming interested in music, Michael Jackson became his idol. His room was covered with posters of him and Donnie used $100 he got for his birthday to buy a red leather jacket like the one Michael Jackson wore. Donnie came in with sunglasses on and wearing the glove. He started to impersonate Michael Jackson's dance moves and singing voice and appeared in shows near where we lived."

Those onstage experiences would be the beginning of a career Donnie hadn't planned on. When he was signed for a new band, New Kids on the Block, right before his fifteenth birthday, new doors opened for him. Donnie proved to his mom that he was able to juggle school, his part-time job at the bank and singing with the group.

All Donnie's high-energy was immediately recognized by fans of the band. "Everyone in the group is full of surprises," he says. "But I'm known as the hyper one. I got that tag because I was always out front at our shows. I had more energy, so I would be the lead."

There are many goals Donnie is looking forward to accomplishing in the years ahead. He already has worked on some outside projects away from the band. Recently, he recorded a duet with Japan's Top Female Vocalist Seiko Matsuda, who has recorded 24 #1 hits in her native country. The song is titled *The Right Combination* and Donnie explains, "It's a great ballad. I was so honored to work with Seiko."

Donnie also produced the new album by the band, The Northside Boys, formerly known as the Boston rap group, One Nation.

When Donnie gets a break from his busy schedule, he likes to go home and relax. "He usually bursts through the door, throws his luggage down and turns on the TV," says his mom. "He'll call his friends to let them know he's home because he's very devoted to his friends."

Donnie often heads to the mall or to a movie. He loves going shopping for new sneakers and playing basketball. Donnie also likes going out with a special girl. "I like females of all races, shapes and sizes," he grins. His favorite thing to do on a date is go for quiet walks and to dinner. "I like being with someone who is kind, trustworthy and will like me for who I am," he says.

Donnie is outgoing, determined, sensitive and caring. His mom says, 'When I think back on him as a child, I would always say, 'He's going to be somebody.' "

Despite his whirlwind success, Donnie has remained down-to-earth and unaffected by stardom. He says it was his mom who has influenced him most. "My mom once told me, 'please do not change,' " he offers. "She said, 'stay the same as you are,' and I think I have."

Q & A with Donnie Wahlberg

Q: What is Donnie's most memorable New Kids moment so far?

A: "Oh, there's so many," smiles Donnie. "I guess the first is when we performed at the Apollo Theater in New York. Another would be the first show we did as a band. We played at a prison in Deer Island, Massachusetts. They loved us. It was pretty wild. As for a personal one, I fell off the stage in Florida. I was so excited about performing that I didn't realize at first I split my finger open and ripped my clothes. That was pretty memorable."

Q: Is there anything Donnie doesn't like about being in the band?

A: Donnie loves being a New Kid, but does admit it is sometimes very stressful. "You don't get too much sleep and sometimes you're real tired," he expresses. "It does get hectic living on the road. You snap at the other guys and it's tough sleeping on the bus. Other times you miss home, eating a home-cooked meal. But on the whole, it's pretty exciting."

Q: What has being a New Kid done for Donnie?

A: "It's just been a great experience and it's helped me to put my life in a good and positive direction," he explains.

Q: What is Donnie's secret wish?

A: One word: Peace. "I'm hoping that everyone could live peacefully together without fear forever," this caring kid says.

Q: How does Donnie feel meeting other celebrities?

A: Since becoming so popular, the New Kids have been introduced to many TV, recording and movie stars. They are always very excited to meet other celebrities. "You know, you watch them on TV or listen to their records and all of a sudden, you're being introduced to them and posing for a picture with them," says Donnie. "I've met a lot of people that I've wanted to meet for a long time."

Donnie's Fact File

Full Real Name: Donald E. Wahlberg, Jr.
Nicknames: Donnie, Dennis Cheese
Birthdate: August 17, 1969
Birthplace: Dorchester, Massachusetts
Hair: Blondish brown
Eyes: Hazel
Height: 5'10"
Weight: 155 lbs.
Shoe Size: 8
Shirt Size: Large
Parents: Donald, Sr. and Alma
Brothers & Sisters: Michelle, Debbie, Paul, Arthur, Jim, Tracey, Bob, Mark
Favorite Breakfast Cereal: Count Chocula
Favorite Drinks: Water, apple juice, Coca-Cola
Favorite Holiday: "My birthday!"
Favorite Cartoon Character: Dennis the Menace
Favorite Sports: Baseball, basketball
Favorite Colors: Black and gold
Favorite Song: *Please Don't Go, Girl*
Favorite Actor: Al Pacino
Favorite Actress: Cher
Favorite Movie: *Scarface*
Favorite Book: *Old Yeller*
Favorite TV Show: *Sesame Street*
Favorite Music: Dance music
Favorite Car: Saab 900 convertible
Favorite Type of Girl: "Someone with a strong personality who likes to have fun and is very independent."
Favorite Type of Date: "Dinner at a quiet restaurant, movie and a walk around Boston. I like it to be just me and my date for a relaxed, private night."
Favorite Type of Clothes: "Leather jackets, sneakers."

Little Known Fact: "I've wanted to be in teen magazines all my life!"
Hobbies: Drawing, dancing
What Makes Donnie Happy: Being on stage
What Makes Donnie Sad: "Losing someone I love"
Instrument Played: Drums
Best Qualities: "I'm kind, giving and tons of fun."
Worst Quality: "I'm very impatient."
Self-Description: "I'm very generous, very serious. I love talking and I'm always thinking. I love to be in love."
Main Goal: "To succeed, but have fun doing it."
Message To Fans: "Peace out! Say No to Drugs!"
Where To Write To Donnie:
Donnie Wahlberg
c/o New Kids on the Block
Columbia Records
51 West 52nd Street
New York, NY 10019

DANNY WOOD

> *"For our first album, we did what Maurice said because we didn't know anything about music. And then with* Hangin' Tough, *we all sat down and decided how we wanted the album to sound."*
> —Danny

Danny Wood never dreamed he'd be part of show business while he was growing up in Boston, Massachusetts. Born on May 14, 1970, black-haired Danny admits that when music entered his life, it completely rearranged his original plans for the future. Danny, who was an A student and had a four-year scholarship to Boston University, wanted to become an architect.

But before he graduated high school, fate played a hand in Danny's life and he was chosen as a band member for the group, New Kids on the Block. Right from the beginning, he loved the idea of being part of the band and started thinking about it all the time. He became interested in engineering and wanted to learn about recording."

"I wanted to do this so bad," he says, "that I really couldn't concentrate on school. I was going to the studio every day learning more and more about engineering. I decided not to go to college

and devote all my time to the New Kids. I still have my scholarship and I know I can go back anytime I want in the future. I feel so lucky to have been chosen for this band and right now, I want to give my all to the group."

Since the New Kids hit it big, Danny has become more and more involved with the band. He is now working behind-the-scenes on the recording; he's written more songs and choreographed some of the guys dance steps in concert. As Danny puts it, "I'm very serious about the New Kids. We're all working hard to make it the best we can."

When he isn't hard at work, the son of Elizabeth and Daniel Wood, Sr. can be found at home in the Dorchester section of Boston, Massachusetts. It is here that Danny unwinds. He shares the old Victorian house with his brothers and sisters and says the Wood clan are all super-close.

When he's got some time to himself,

Danny likes to spend it with friends. "We usually go to a local dance club or play basketball or soccer," he says.

He'll also go see a horror movie with his friends because "they're my favorite kind of movies even if they do scare me sometimes." Danny doesn't often admit his sensitive side, like the fact that he travels with his favorite teddy bear and admits to being a little superstitious.

This brown-eyed guy gives off the impression of being super cool during a New Kids concert. But don't let him "kid" you. Danny does get nervous once in a while. It is the audience who will put Danny at ease right away.

He remembers one funny experience during one of their shows with Tiffany. "We didn't have cordless microphones and the cords were everywhere," he begins. "Jordan began to sing his lead part on *The Right Stuff* when I stepped right on my mike cord, which made it real tight—and my mike went flying out into the audience!"

Right now, Danny is learning to play the piano and has been practicing whenever he has some extra time. His interests range from songwriting to engineering to performing. "We've been so lucky," he says with a warm smile. "Someday, I'd like to be able to help other kids get started in this business. I want to make other kids' dreams come true the way mine have!"

Danny's Fact File

Full Real Name: Daniel William Wood, Jr.
Nicknames: Puff McCloud, Woody Woodpecker
Birthdate: May 14, 1970
Birthplace: Boston, Massachusetts

Hair: Black
Eyes: Brown
Height: 5'8"
Weight: 145 lbs.
Shoe Size: 8½
Shirt Size: Medium
Parents: Daniel, Sr. and Elizabeth
Brothers & Sisters: Bethany, Pam, Brett, Rachel, Melissa
Favorite Actor: Kevin Costner
Favorite Actress: Cher
Favorite Movies: *Stand By Me, Star Wars, The Terminator*
Favorite TV Show: *The Cosby Show*
Favorite Foods: Roast beef, Chinese, Italian, chicken
Favorite Drink: Water
Favorite Snack: Fruit
Favorite Car: Cherokee Jeep
Favorite Sport: Basketball
Favorite Song: *Some Things Never Change* by The Stylistics
Favorite Vacation Spot: Florida
Favorite Holiday: Christmas
Favorite Cartoon Character: Woody Woodpecker
Favorite Type of Girl: "Someone cute, easygoing, nice and funny."
Favorite Type of Date: "Just spending time with a special girl talking and getting to know each other."
Scariest Childhood Memory: Falling off his bicycle.
Main Goals: To be successful
Self-Description: "Stubborn, easygoing, determined."
Worst Habit: Getting defensive
Pet Peeve: Prejudice
Future Plans: "I want to be a top recording engineer, but first I'd like to see the New Kids record lots of platinum albums."
Message To Fans: "Be happy, stay off the streets and hold onto your dreams. Someday they just may come true."
Where To Write To Danny:
Danny Wood
c/o New Kids on the Block
Columbia Records
51 West 52nd Street
New York, NY 10019

Part Two •••••••••••••

NEW KIDS' RISE TO FAME

Summer, 1984: Producer/songwriter Maurice Starr and manager Mary Alford, who had formed the successful black group New Edition, wanted to start a streetwise white group with a black sound. In a city-wide talent search held in Boston, Massachusetts, they began auditioning for five young guys who could sing, dance and rap.

Six months later, Donnie Wahlberg was the first member chosen for the band. Donnie, who with his five brothers were known as the legendary Boston "tough guys", was famous for his Michael Jackson impersonations.

Maurice Starr saw a lot of potential in Donnie and knew his raw talent could be polished with a little work. "When I was signed up, I contacted Jon and Jordan Knight because I remembered them from school," says Donnie. "We had gone to the William Monroe Trotter School in Boston. I told them about the group and convinced them to try out. Then I talked Danny into auditioning."

With four members selected, Donnie persuaded another friend, Jamie Kelly, to audition. He was also chosen, but his parents decided they didn't want him to be part of show business at a young age. When he dropped out, the last and youngest "kid" chosen for the group was Joe McIntyre.

With the band finally completed, Starr began writing and arranging songs. He had the group record four songs on a demo which he shipped to major record labels in the last half of 1985. The band, which at the time was named Nynuk, was signed to a recording contract with Columbia records in January, 1986.

Their only problem was the group's moniker. "Our record company didn't like it because they thought it sounded too much like Menudo," says Joe. Wanting to change their name, they recorded one of their first rap tunes called New Kids on the Block. It seemed perfect and the five-member band from Boston *became* New Kids on the Block.

It was clear they were on their way, but still had a lot of hard work ahead of them. They released their first single *Be My Girl* in April, 1986. It was a hit with dance club D.J.'s but before the kids released their debut album, they joined the July 4th Statue of Liberty festivities.

As part of the "City Kids Speak on Liberty" at Battery Park, they performed for thousands of enthusiastic fans. They also opened for the Four Tops at the Kite Festival and for Lisa Lisa and Cult Jam at a club in Boston.

The New Kids would release two more singles off their first album, *Stop It Girl* and a remake of the Delfonics 1970 Philly soul

classic *Didn't I (Blow Your Mind)*, but the album wasn't the success they had hoped it would be.

This disappointing news didn't stop the New Kids; instead it pushed them to do better. They started writing songs and working on new dance routines for what was to become *Hangin' Tough*.

One thing taken into account while working on new material was the growth in experience and maturity that the five had gone through since the beginnings of the band. "We're growing up," states Jon, "And we have to have a more grown-up image now."

For their second album, *Hangin' Tough*, the group decided to change their sound. "For the first album we did basically what Maurice said, because we didn't know anything about music," says Danny. "With *Hangin' Tough*, we all sat down and decided how we wanted the album to sound, and if Maurice brought in a bad song, we would say we didn't want to do it. We didn't really think consciously to have an older sound. It just happened that way.

"We definitely were teenyboppers with our first album," continues Danny. "But as far as *Hangin' Tough*, most of the music could have been sung by anybody, no matter what age they are."

Donnie says, "*Hangin' Tough*, in our eyes, is the symbol of us . . . of what we are."

The release of R&B, pop ballads and dance hits like *Please Don't Go Girl, I'll Be Loving You (Forever), You Got It (The Right Stuff), Hangin' Tough* and *Cover Girl* off the album put the New Kids on top.

At the Boston Music Awards on Tuesday, April 25, 1989, the New Kids walked away with quite a few awards including "Outstanding Music Video" and "Outstanding R&B Single for *You Got It (The Right Stuff)*" and Maurice Starr was named "Producer of the Year."

The Boston Herald raved, "Forget Bobby Brown. Forget Tracey Chapman. Tuesday night's ceremony for the third annual Boston Music Awards belonged to five teens from Dorchester—New Kids on the Block, who put on a performance before the hometown fans that literally shook the Wang Center. They sang, danced and strutted . . . and kept the young female fans, who made up the majority of the crowd, screaming with delight."

Hangin' Tough was Billboard's second best-selling album of 1989. The album passed the RIAA double-platinum mark and sold over 4 million copies to date. They tied a record set by Diana Ross in 1980. The New Kids had three songs in the Top 40 at the same time with *Hangin' Tough, Cover Girl* and the re-release of *Didn't I (Blow Your Mind)*.

The New Kids never stop working. In between their sold-out concerts, they appeared in record stores to sign copies of their albums for over 5,000 eager fans. Their worldwide popularity has taken them across the United States and to Japan, England and Australia. In Japan, they met fans, gave interviews to magazines, performed one electrifying show and filmed a commercial for a CD player. While in England, they appeared on *The Disney Club* and drove the crowds wild.

Here are the New Kids with their parents. All five guys say they couldn't have done it without the support of their families.

During a stop in Detroit, the band hosted Nickelodeon's "Block Party," beginning at the contest winner's home and continuing at a bowling alley outside the city. The New Kids returned to the Motor City to take over West Utica Elementary School for the day. It was later broadcast on the Nickelodeon cable channel.

Because of their popularity, they were chosen to host the Second Annual Dance Music Awards, held at the Universal Amphitheatre in Los Angeles on February 12, 1990. And they performed Smokey Robinson's classic songs as part of a tribute to Robinson on the *Grammy Living Legends* television special.

But, probably the most exciting night for New Kids on the Block was winning two American Music Awards on January 22, 1989. The Kids walked away with the award for "Best Pop/Rock Group" and "Best Pop/Rock Album-*Hangin' Tough.*"

In his acceptance speech, Donnie summed up the band's super success by first saying, "not bad for five guys from Dorchester." He brought producer Maurice Starr onstage and said, "Without him having his dream, we couldn't have had our dreams come true."

Then, with a smile, Donnie added, "Music truly is the universal and international language even if it's spoken with a Boston accent."

With their good looks, easygoing personalities and undeniable talent, this quintet has taken over as the world's most popular teen heartthrobs. And the guys are enjoying every minute they spend on the road, meeting fans and signing autographs.

Of the band's name, Jon says, "We've already talked about how we're going to feel five or ten years from now especially being called New Kids on the Block. By then, we won't be so new anymore. I've

New Kids on the Block were guests on England's TV show, The Disney Club.

talked to our producer and record company about what we should do about changing the name. They told me maybe they'll change it. We'll have to wait and see."

The New Kids are set to star in their first movie and there's talk of taking the band to Saturday morning in cartoon form.

According to Donnie: "There is a wide open field for New Kids on the Block in the future. I see Joe maybe doing TV. I see myself doing some acting or getting into rap. I see Jordan producing. I see Jonathan as a business manager, some type of behind-the-scenes role in the music business. I see Danny becoming a songwriter or recording engineer."

But looking ahead will have to wait. These five music stars take it day by day. Right now, they are focusing on their current success at the top of the pop charts.

You can see what close friends Joe and Jon really are.

Part Three•••••••••••••
NEW KIDS IN CONCERT

If the New Kids had to choose one thing they like best about being in the band, these five hip hit-makers all admit that performing live onstage is the most fun of all.

"There's nothing to compare it with in the world. It's the greatest thrill!" enthuses Donnie.

New Kids on the Block gained their experience by playing in the Boston area. Thinking back to the band's first concert, Jon says, "We were all a little nervous the first time we went onstage. But we all got used to it fast."

It was a challenge for the New Kids in the beginning. Every night they'd get onstage and try to prove themselves to the audiences. "People would look at us and think we were just some kids trying to get on a tour," says Donnie. "But as soon as we'd start singing, we'd win the audience over. For me, it was like a mission every night to tear the roof down!"

Their big break came in the summer of 1988 when they were signed as the opening act for Tiffany. The New Kids caught on instantly and were soon headlining their own shows.

Danny, who choreographs some of the New Kids dance steps, says, "When they give our shows a lot of hype, I feel those butterflies in my stomach."

Each of the New Kids gets a chance at singing lead except Jon, who feels "I'm not ready for it yet." Instead he harmonizes here with fellow bandmember Joe.

At every electrifying concert, they send their audience into a frenzy. As soon as these five kids appear onstage and start rocking the house, the entire audience erupts into cheers and screams. And it doesn't let up until the show is over.

Everyone who has gone to a New Kids concert has gone home completely satisfied. The guys make their fans feel very welcome by acknowledging them as they perform. Donnie, who comes right up to the edge of the stage when he sings lead, says, "I'm always winking at a girl or waving at someone when we perform."

Jon uses his time spent onstage to make his fans know how much he really cares about them. Sometimes because of their hectic schedules, the guys can't always meet as many fans as they'd like to. "Sometimes I'll look out into the audience and look straight into someone's eyes and smile. I like them to know I'm there for them," says Jon.

A New Kids concert seems to be more like a party than a show. It's the time when the audience and Jon, Jordan, Joe, Donnie and Danny get together for one night of fun. These guys definitely have the right stuff especially when they're singing, rapping and dancing onstage.

"When I'm onstage, I get real intense and real serious," says Donnie.

Jordan performs for thousands of New Kids fans.

"We really love our fans," says Joe. "It's the best part of being in the business."

"When the crowd reacts with screams, claps and waves," says Danny, "then that's succeeding!"

"Everywhere we go, we meet a lot of people," says Jon. "We end up making friends in every city we travel to."

Part Four

DIARY OF FABULOUS FACTS

All five guys agree that the thing that makes them most happy is Peace on Earth.

The most exciting moment for Joe, Jordan, Jon, Danny and Donnie was performing at the Apollo Theater in New York.

Jon describes himself as "confident, but not conceited."

Jordan's professional ambition is "to become a songwriter and producer."

The New Kids have been called "a modernized version of the Osmonds."

"Kids relate to us because we've got a lot of energy and excitement," offers Jordan.

The guys performed at London's Wembley Stadium in fall, 1989 with George Michael and Tina Turner.

Jordan plays keyboards but he's also learning how to play the guitar.

The New Kids lend their time and support to many charity events, including Say No To Drugs foundation.

Jordan's biggest fear is the supernatural.

Danny says his best quality is "I don't crack under pressure."

Donnie was named after his dad. His full name is Donald E. Wahlberg, Jr.

The video for the single *I'll Be Loving You (Forever)* was filmed at a Brooklyn, New York school in April, 1989.

Jon likes to swim and ski.

Jordan's favorite car is a Porsche.

Donnie's mom bought him his very first earring and now he wears four earrings in his left ear.

One hundred and eighty thousand New Kids schoolbook covers were distributed to students nationwide via 80 CHR/Gavin stations.

If Joe had one wish, he says he'd like to end homelessness.

Jon likes Mickey Mouse.

The New Kids have been dubbed "The Five Hardest Working Kids in Show Business."

Donnie's biggest dislike is "people judging me without knowing me."

The first record Danny bought was *Let's Dance* by David Bowie.

"Being a New Kid is the best learning experience you could ever have," says Jordan.

On hot summer days, Donnie reaches for a cold bottle of Coca-Cola.

Jon plays the saxophone.

The video for the single *You Got It (The Right Stuff)* was filmed on location in Louisiana in the fall of 1988.

Jordan can't shake the habit of biting his nails.

While traveling, Donnie and Jon take their pillows from home, while Joe brings along his teddy bear.

In September, 1989, the New Kids visited England and appeared on *The Disney Club*.

Jordan puts ketchup on everything, including eggs.

Donnie is left-handed.

The New Kids appeared on *Dance Party, U.S.A.* on May 18, 1989.

Joe is the youngest "kid."

The New Kids helped Tiffany celebrate her 18th birthday in October, 1989 at a party held at Universal Studios in Hollywood.

Donnie says "the New Kids came together by destiny."

The New Kids appeared on the Sunday morning kids' show, *Steampipe Alley,* on April 9, 1989.

Danny's first ambition was to be an architect.

When Joe's sister Judith was appearing in the play *Peg Of My Heart* in New York, he was unable to go see her. At the time, Joe was also in New York, but performing with the New Kids. So he sent his sister a dozen roses at the theater and a card wishing her good luck.

Donnie loves munching on *Mike and Ike's* candies.

Joe has a talent for remembering the smallest details.

The New Kids and all their brothers and sisters add up to a total of 30.

The New Kids filmed the video of their single *This One's for the Children* at the Empire Stages Studio in Queens, New York.

When the guys were in London, Jordan pierced both his ears.

Donnie's older brother, Bob, says, "I don't think Donnie is the type who will ever forget about his family and friends no matter how popular he gets. He's the kind of guy who cares about everyone and everything."

Jon is a fan of Kirk Cameron, the star of the television series *Growing Pains*. Says Jon, "Now there's a guy I want to meet."

Danny's older sister, Pam, recently moved out of the Wood household. Danny, who had been sharing a bedroom with his younger brother, moved into his sister's old room. "Finally," he exclaims, "I have my own bedroom."

Joe's favorite Christmas present "was a Batman Big Wheel I got when I was five years old."

Donnie bought a new home near Boston for his mom, Alma.

The New Kids are the teen spokesmen for United Cerebral Palsy foundation. Last spring, they took part in the UCP bike-a-thon in New York City.

The New Kids donate part of the proceeds from their 900 hotline number to United Cerebral Palsy foundation.

Jordan says his mother and producer Maurice Starr have been the two biggest influences on his life "because they taught me to shoot for the best!"

Jon's favorite holiday is Easter.

Donnie's worst habit is "eating too much junk food."

Jordan's personal ambition "is to have fun."

Danny's most prized moments are "the time I spend with my mom!"

Joe plays the tambourine.

Jordan and Danny were both born in the month of May.

The New Kids did a commercial for a portable radio/CD player in Japan.

The New Kids travel to their concert dates in a tour bus.

Donnie's favorite food "is my dad's home cooking and Kentucky Fried Chicken."

Jon is nicknamed *GQ* (after the men's fashion magazine) because he loves shopping for new clothes.

Danny, Donnie, Jon and Jordan were all classmates at the William Monroe Trotter School in Boston.

The New Kids always travel with bodyguards.

Donnie's first ambition was to be a baseball player.

Jordan sports a unique hairstyle—he has a side part and a long braid.

"I think we always knew we could be successful," says Donnie, "but when it finally came it was a big surprise."

New Kids Notes

My favorite New Kid is _____

because _____

_____

_____

_____

_____

_____

_____

_____

_____

_____

_____

_____

_____

_____

_____

_____

_____

_____

_____

_____

_____

_____

_____

_____

_____

_____

_____

Pose With New Kids

Place Your Photo Here

Part Five

NEW KIDS' TRIVIA QUIZ

Multiple Choice

1. Which New Kid sang lead on the song, *I'll Be Loving You Forever?*
   - A) Jon
   - B) Jordan
   - C) Joe

2. Which New Kid co-wrote the song, *Funky, Funky Xmas* with producer Maurice Starr?
   - A) Jordan
   - B) Danny
   - C) Donnie

3. Danny's favorite car is:
   - A) BMW
   - B) Saab
   - C) Cherokee Jeep

4. Jon and what other New Kid had a crush on the same girl when they were in the sixth grade?
   - A) Jordan
   - B) Donnie
   - C) Danny

5. Which New Kid played the title role in the musical play, *Oliver?*
   - A) Joe
   - B) Danny
   - C) Jordan

True or False

6. Jon once won an award for writing a Christmas story about Santa Claus.

7. The New Kids add "izz" to the first letter of each of their names.

8. Donnie likes the colors black and red.

9. Joe's mother, Kay, is afraid to fly in airplanes.

10. Jordan loves vanilla milkshakes.

Fill in the Blanks

11. The only blue-eyed member of the group is _____.

12. Jordan has two siamese cats named _____.

13. _____, _____ and _____ are the three New Kids who write and co-produce under the name Crickets.

14. Danny was born under the astrological sign _____.

15. _____ is the shyest member of the group.

DISCOGRAPHY

New Kids Singles

Be My Girl
Stop It Girl
Didn't I (Blow Your Mind)
Please Don't Go Girl
You Got It (The Right Stuff)
Hangin' Tough
Didn't I (Blow Your Mind)—rereleased
Cover Girl
This One's For the Children

New Kids Albums

New Kids on the Block (Columbia, 1986;
    rereleased, 1989)
Tracks:
Stop It Girl
Didn't I (Blow Your Mind)
Popsicle
Angel
Be My Girl
New Kids on the Block
Are You Down?
I Wanna Be Loved By You
Don't Give Up On Me
Treat Me Right

New Kids on the Block—Hangin' Tough
    (Columbia, 1988)
Tracks:
You Got It (The Right Stuff)
Please Don't Go Girl
I'll Be Loving You (Forever)
Cover Girl

I Need You
Hangin' Tough
I Remember When
What'Cha Gonna Do (About It)
My Favorite Girl
Hold On

*New Kids on the Block—Merry, Merry
    Christmas* (Columbia, 1989)
Tracks:
This One's For the Children
Last Night I Saw Santa Claus
I'll Be Missin' You Come Christmas
    (A Letter to Santa)
I Still Believe in Santa Claus
Merry, Merry Christmas
The Christmas Song (Chestnuts Roasting
    on an Open Fire)
Funky, Funky Xmas
White Christmas
Little Drummer Boy
This One's For the Children (Reprise)